TIME TRA███████ES

█IENT

█YPT

Liz Gogerly

www.raintree.co.uk/library
Visit our website to find out more information about Raintree books.

To order:

☎ Phone 44 (0) 1865 888112

📄 Send a fax to 44 (0) 1865 314091

💻 Visit the Raintree bookshop at www.raintree.co.uk/library to browse our catalogue and order online.

First published in Great Britain by Raintree, Halley Court, Jordan Hill, Oxford OX2 8EJ, part of Harcourt Education. Raintree is a registered trademark of Harcourt Education Ltd.

© Harcourt Education Ltd 2007
First published in paperback in 2008
The moral right of the proprietor has been asserted.

Editorial: Sarah Shannon, Lucy Beevor, and Harriet Milles
Design: Steve Mead and Geoff Ward
Picture Research: Ruth Blair
Illustrations: Eikon Illustration & Tim Slade
Production: Duncan Gilbert

Originated by Modern Age
Printed and bound in China by South China Printing Company Limited

10 digit ISBN 1 4062 0600 8 (hardback)
13 digit ISBN 978 1 4062 0600 5

11 10 09 08 07
10 9 8 7 6 5 4 3 2 1

10-digit ISBN1 4062 0607 5 (paperback)
13-digit ISBN 978 1 4062 0607 4

11 10 09 08
10 9 8 7 6 5 4 3 2 1

British Library Cataloguing in Publication Data
Gogerly, Liz
Ancient Egypt. - (Time travel guides)
1. Egypt - Civilization - To 332 B.C. - Juvenile literature
932'.01
A full catalogue record for this book is available from the British Library.

Acknowledgements
The publishers would like to thank the following for permission to reproduce photographs:
AKG Images **pp. 58–59** (Archives CDA; Guillot), **11**, **54–55** (Erich Lessing), **6–7** (Herve Champollion), **41** (Suzanne Held); Alamy **p. 34** (Gary Cook); Ancient Art & Architecture Collection Ltd. **pp. 44–45** (Mary Jelliffe), **25** (Ronald Sheridan), **12** (Y. Shishido), **23, 38, 39, 40, 48–49**; Art Archive **pp. 36** (Bibliothèque Musée du Louvre/Dagli Orti), **42–43** (British Museum, London/Dagli Orti), **9, 20, 29, 37, 40, 47** (Egyptian Museum, Cairo/Dagli Orti), **13, 14, 18–19, 21, 28, 46, 53** (Dagli Orti), **58–59** (Egyptian Museum, Turin/Dagli Orti), **16** (Khawam Collection, Paris/Dagli Orti), **15, 17, 21, 22, 30, 44** (Musée du Louvre, Paris/Dagli Orti), **51** (Ragab Papyrus Institute, Cairo/Dagli Orti), **32–33**; Corbis **pp. 26–27** (Frans Lemmens/Zefa), **31** (Jose Fuste Raga).

Cover images of a necklace with winged scarab pectoral from Tutankhamen's treasure, and Cuff bracelet with eye Oudjat from the tomb of Sheshonq II, 930 BC, reproduced with permission of Ancient Art & Architecture Collection Ltd. Cover photograph of the Sphinx reproduced with permission of Getty Images/ Photodisc.

The publishers would like to thank Christina Riggs for her assistance in the preparation of this book.

Every effort has been made to contact copyright holders of any material reproduced in this book. Any omissions will be rectified in subsequent printings if notice is given to the publishers.

CONTENTS

Words that appear in the text in bold, **like this**, are explained in the Glossary.

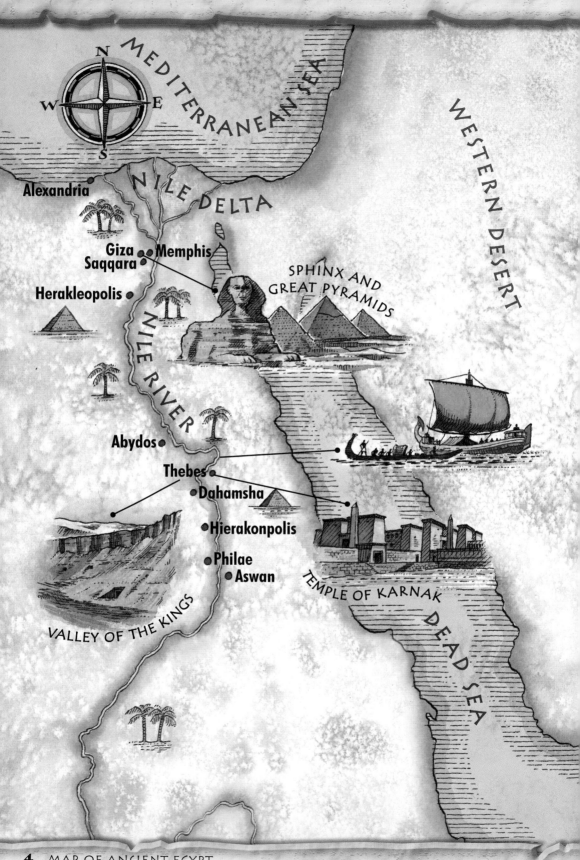

MEDITERRANEAN SEA

WESTERN DESERT

N
W E
S

NILE DELTA

Alexandria

Giza • Memphis
Saqqara

Herakleopolis

SPHINX AND
GREAT PYRAMIDS

NILE RIVER

Abydos

Thebes

Dahamsha

Hierakonpolis

Philae
Aswan

TEMPLE OF KARNAK

DEAD SEA

VALLEY OF THE KINGS

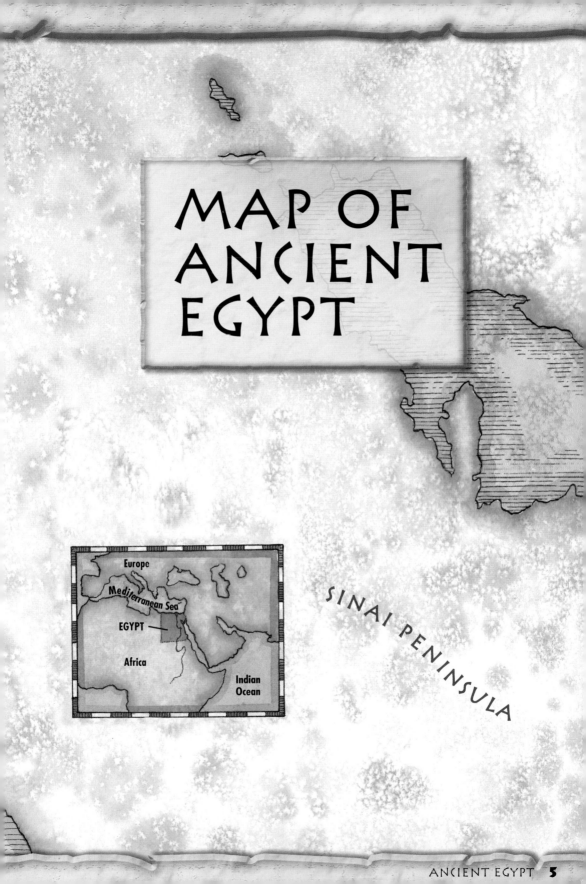

MAP OF ANCIENT EGYPT

Europe

Mediterranean Sea

EGYPT

Africa

Indian Ocean

SINAI PENINSULA

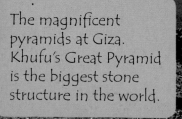

The magnificent pyramids at Giza. Khufu's Great Pyramid is the biggest stone structure in the world.

CHAPTER 1

FACTS ABOUT ANCIENT EGYPT

Ancient Egypt is like no other place on Earth so it is best to plan your trip well. You will be fascinated by the pyramids and tombs which are burial sites for pharaohs. The weather is often very hot and dry but seek out the shade and you will be rewarded with a trip of a lifetime.

This section helps you find the best times to visit and when you should avoid going. As well as information about the weather you will also find out more about the politics, culture, and beliefs of the people of this intriguing ancient country.

WHEN TO TRAVEL

Ancient Egypt has a long and colourful history, spanning more than 3,000 years. Its history has been divided into major periods, and then into dynasties. A dynasty tends to be the time that one family or group of pharaohs (kings) ruled ancient Egypt.

TIMELINE OF ANCIENT EGYPT

(Note: dates given are approximate.)

EARLY DYNASTIC PERIOD (3100–2686 BC)
1st Dynasty
   Narmer (3100 BC)
OLD KINGDOM (2686–2181 BC)
4th Dynasty
   Khufu (2589–2566 BC)
   Khafre (2558–2532 BC)
FIRST INTERMEDIATE PERIOD (2181–2055 BC)
MIDDLE KINGDOM (2055–1650 BC)
11th Dynasty
   Mentuhotep II (2055–2004 BC)
SECOND INTERMEDIATE PERIOD (1650–1550 BC)
NEW KINGDOM (1550–1069 BC)
18th Dynasty
   Amenhotep II (1427–1400 BC)
   Ramesses II (1279–1213 BC)
THIRD INTERMEDIATE PERIOD (1069–747 BC)

Key:
- Stay away
- Okay times to visit
- Best times to visit

EARLY TIMES

A good time to visit is during the Early Dynastic Period, when Egypt becomes a united country for the first time. King Narmer (sometimes known as Menes) of Upper Egypt has just defeated the ruler of Lower Egypt. Narmer is the founder of the first dynasty of ancient Egyptian rulers.

OLD KINGDOM

Arrive during the Old Kingdom and you should head for the centre of power in Memphis. Complete your trip with a day at the great pyramids of Khufu and Khafre at Giza.

MIDDLE KINGDOM

If you're looking for peace and quiet, try to plan your trip for the final years of the reign of Mentuhotep II. After years of civil war he has brought peace back to ancient Egypt and is building an amazing temple just below the cliffs at Deir el-Bahri near the **capital** Thebes.

NEW KINGDOM

During this time, Egypt is the most powerful **empire** in the ancient world. A visit during the reign of Amenhotep II is highly recommended. Ancient Egyptian art is at its all-time best. You can admire the wall paintings, sculptures, and beautifully decorated jewellery. Many of these works of art are buried with the dead. You'll be able to sneak a look before they are sealed away from human eyes for thousands of years.

WHEN NOT TO TRAVEL

- During the First Intermediate Period when Egypt is shaken by war, national unrest, **plague**, and (later) foreign invasion.
- In the Second Intermediate Period when the **Hyksos** have taken control of parts of ancient Egypt.
- By the Third Intermediate Period and the Late Period, much of ancient Egypt has been ruled by the Assyrians, the Persians, the Libyans, the Nubians, and the Greeks.

Ramesses II ("The Great") (1279–1213 BC) was a strong ruler of the New Kingdom. His reign would be another good time to visit.

GEOGRAPHY AND CLIMATE

The River Nile dominates the landscape of ancient Egypt. It flows northwards for over 965 km (600 miles) before it spreads out to form a **delta**. The land next to the river is beautiful and green. From high up the delta looks like the back of a triangular leaf covered with veins. These "veins" are hundreds of streams and water channels which flow into the blue-green Mediterranean Sea.

RED AND BLACK LAND

The ancient Egyptians call the lush strip of land surrounding the Nile *Kemet*, or "Black Land". It is named after the rich black **silt** that is washed up by the Nile when it floods each year. They call the desert beyond *Deshret*, or "Red Land". The change from fertile land to desert is rather sudden. It is even possible to put one foot on the "Black Land" and the other on the "Red Land".

LAND OF THE NILE

The Greek historian Herodotus (about 484–425 BC) said "Egypt is the gift of her river."

THE SEASONS OF THE NILE

The Nile even makes the seasons. From July to October the fields surrounding the Nile are flooded. The farmers can't work on the flooded fields so they find other work instead. Some of them work as builders. From November to February the farmers are back in the fields. You will see them busily ploughing and sowing. In March to June the farmers harvest their crops. This is the best time to sample fresh fruit and vegetables.

TEMPERATURES IN THE NILE VALLEY

July/August: temperature is between 25–40 °C (77–104 °F).

January: the coolest month with temperatures between 8–24 °C (46–75 °F).

There is little rainfall all over the country, but expect a few drops in winter around the Nile Delta.

Most of ancient Egypt's population is found on the **fertile** land surrounding the Nile. The people rely upon the river for drinking water, agriculture, fish, trade, and communication.

GOOD NILE OR BAD NILE?

You will often hear the locals talk about "a good Nile" or "a bad Nile". They are talking about how good the floods have been. "A good Nile" means that the Nile has flooded the fields along its banks and there will be a good harvest. If it's "a bad Nile" then perhaps the river didn't flood. This could mean that the farmers don't have enough water for their crops and there may be famine.

CUSTOMS AND CULTURE

"GOD-KING"

Most rulers in ancient Egypt are men, called pharaohs, but there are some queens, such as Queen Hatshepsut. Egyptians think the pharaoh is a descendent of the early gods. They believe he has control over everyday things, such as the flooding of the Nile. It is the custom in ancient Egypt to kiss the ground the pharaoh has walked on!

WHAT DO YOU CALL THE PHARAOH?

If you happen to meet the pharaoh then it is polite to call him "your majesty". During the period of the New Kingdom, people called the king *pr-aa*, which means "great house". This is where the word pharaoh comes from.

GOVERNMENT

The pharaoh has complete control over the running of the country. Second to the pharaoh is a kind of prime minister, called a **vizier**. He is the pharaoh's advisor but he also acts as treasurer, **high priest**, and **chief justice**. There is also a whole network of officials who run different departments of government.

CLASS SYSTEM

At the top of the class system in ancient Egypt are the pharaoh and royal family. Next there are the **aristocracy** and important people, such as the vizier. Government officials and priests also rank highly.

The pharaohs of ancient Egypt wear a false beard. It helps to make them look intelligent and wise.

Next come administrators, **scribes**, and rich land owners. The largest sector of society comes at the bottom and includes, in order of importance, soldiers, skilled and manual workers, peasant farmers, servants, and slaves. People don't complain about their position, as they believe that the gods decide a person's place in society.

WOMEN

Women from important or wealthy families in ancient Egypt have many rights. They can inherit property, run businesses, and become priestesses. People believe that the mother and wife of the pharaoh are divine and should be treated with respect.

A scribe uses a reed and a palette for writing. They usually use red and black ink.

However, women from lower down the social scale are treated as second-class citizens. They are expected to obey their husband and give him lots of children. Many women stay at home and run the household. Some women do work outside the home, acting as servants or doing jobs like weaving, baking, brewing, and farming.

CHILDREN

Families in ancient Egypt like to have lots of children. Only the boys of wealthy families go to school. Many children have to work. They often help their parents with farming, weaving, and brewing.

Children can marry in ancient Egypt. Girls often marry as young as 12 years old and boys get married at 14 years old. This is because life expectancy is very low in ancient Egypt. Most people cannot expect to live much longer than 40 years.

RELIGION

Religion is very important to ancient Egyptians. They worship many different gods and goddesses. They believe the gods have power over everything, including the size of this year's harvest, the weather, and the sex of a newborn baby.

KEEPING THE BALANCE

One of the most important parts of the religion of ancient Egyptians is about keeping order and balance in the universe. Ancient Egyptians believe the universe is made up of many opposites such as birth and death, flooding and drought, and order and chaos. Most ancient Egyptians are petrified of chaos. They believe that it is their responsibility to keep balance within the world.

A colourful **papyrus**, called the Dendara Zodiac, shows many of the gods and goddesses of ancient Egypt.

PLEASING MA'AT

The goddess of Universal Order is Ma'at. The pharaoh pleases Ma'at by performing rituals to all the gods at the temple each day. Everybody else pleases Ma'at by keeping balance in their lives, obeying the pharaoh, and being honest and just.

A GOD FOR EVERYTHING

There are well over 2,000 gods in ancient Egypt. The gods can be in human or animal form, or a strange mixture of both! There are national gods, which means they are worshipped by people all over the country. A popular national god is the sun god, Re (or Amun-Re). On wall-paintings Re is usually a falcon, a ram, or a man with a falcon or ram's head. There are also many local gods that are worshipped by people living in one area.

OTHER GODS TO LOOK OUT FOR...

- **Anubis** – The god of **mummification** (see page 16–17). He watches over priests as they **embalm** dead bodies. In art he is represented by a jackal or a man with a jackal's head.
- **Hathor** – Goddess of love, children, music, and dance. In pictures she is usually shown as a cow.
- **Horus** – The ancient god of the sky and the son of Osiris and Isis. Horus is usually represented by a falcon.
- **Osiris** – Husband and brother of Isis, and god of the underworld. In art he appears in human form with a crown of reeds and ostrich feathers, carrying a crook and flail.
- **Thoth** – The god of wisdom and the Moon. On paintings he appears as an ibis or baboon.
- **Isis** – The greatest goddess of all, and the mother of Horus. She is the guardian of children and has amazing magical powers. In art she appears as a woman.

Horus

Osiris

Thoth

TEMPLES

Temples are not places where you can go to worship. These magnificent buildings are believed to be the home of the god to whom it is dedicated. A statue of the god is kept inside the inner chamber, the most holy part of the temple. The temples are run by priests and priestesses, who perform special ceremonies and rituals to the god each day. Some temples are dedicated to the honour of a dead ruler.

Ordinary people are not allowed inside any of these temples. However, the buildings are truly impressive from the outside, so they are certainly worth a visit. The most outstanding temple complexes can be found at Karnak and Luxor (see pages 38–39).

An ancient Egyptian amulet with the Eye of Horus. People wear charms like this to protect them from evil.

WAYS OF WORSHIP

The outside walls of some temples are decorated with the ears of the god to whom they are dedicated. These are called "chapels of the hearing ear". If you see people whispering into temple walls it may look odd, but they are simply saying their prayers into the ear of the god.

Others worship by visiting small shrines dedicated to a certain god. You will see these **shrines** everywhere with offerings of food, flowers, and gifts. Ordinary people also make small shrines at home. These can be dedicated to the gods or to the spirit of a family member who has died.

MAGIC MOMENTS

The ancient Egyptians believe in magic. When a woman is going to have a baby she chants spells to the gods Bes, Taweret, and Hathor, asking them to protect her and the baby. People also wear magic charms or **amulets** to ward off sickness and evil.

ANCIENT MUMMIES

The ancient Egyptians want to continue living forever. They believe that a corpse should be preserved for the **Afterlife**. Ordinary people are usually laid to rest in the desert where their body is dried by the sand and naturally **mummified**. They are then buried with some possessions (food, jewellery, amulets) they may need in the next life.

Royalty and the **elite** are mummified in a more elaborate way. The process of mummification takes 70 days from the moment of death. First of all the lungs, stomach, liver, and intestines are removed. Then the corpse is packed with special salt. When the body is dried out the salt is removed and the corpse is stuffed with resin and linen. Afterwards the body is covered in oil and perfume. Finally, the corpse is wrapped in linen bandages and laid to rest in a large stone coffin, called a **sarcophagus**. The coffin is sealed away in a tomb with food and belongings, such as furniture, fine clothes, and jewellery, that will be needed in the Afterlife.

A tomb painting showing the god of mummification, Anubis (the jackal god), performing a ritual during the burial of a pharaoh.

This painted decoration from an 18th Dynasty nobleman's tomb shows servants bearing offerings of geese, corn, and fine wine.

CHAPTER 2

PRACTICAL INFORMATION

Egypt is very hot so you need to pack plenty of suitable clothing for your visit. If you don't want to stand out in the crowd then take lots of white clothes. On the food front, there is delicious fresh fruit and vegetables to sample, as well as the national dish of goose. And everyone drinks beer, including children! On a practical note, the ancient Egyptians don't use money, so read on to find out how you are going to make the most of your shopping trips.

WHAT TO WEAR

The ancient Egyptians have hardly changed the way they dress for thousands of years! They have always worn white linen, as it is lightweight and feels cool.

All men wear a kind of apron or kilt. It can be tied at the front or with two knots on either hip. In later times the fashion is for pleated kilts with fringes at the edges. Men also tend to wear a kind of tunic-style shirt.

Women look elegant in their straight sheath-like dresses, which are tied behind the neck or at each shoulder. On cool evenings most women wear a shawl. Slaves and servants sometimes wear clothes made from patterned fabric. Children dress much like their parents or they wear nothing at all. People mostly go barefoot, but the rich sometimes wear sandals made of leather or reeds.

JEWELLERY

Ancient Egyptian jewellery is colourful and eye-catching. People wear jewelled rings, anklets, bracelets, earrings, necklaces, collars, belts, and headdresses. The very rich can afford precious metals and jewels but the poor make do with pottery beads. The ancient Egyptians make some of the most striking jewellery in the ancient world, which makes it an ideal gift to take home to loved ones.

A fine example of a precious amulet. At the centre is the scarab beetle, said to symbolize rebirth.

FINISHING TOUCHES

The ancient Egyptians spend a lot of time trying to look good. Make-up isn't just for women – men use it too. Most people use a black dye called kohl as eye-liner. Then they apply eye shadows – powdered malachite (a bright-green mineral) is very popular.

If you want to be fashionable in ancient Egypt then wearing white is a must.

An ancient Egyptian girl with a woven wig. Beeswax is used to set the style.

Wigs are very popular amongst the upper classes. They help protect them from sunstroke. Women's hairstyles tend to be long and straight. Braids and jewels are sometimes added. Many people also shave off all their body hair. Children have short hair, often with a sidelock (a long lock of hair) on the right-hand side of their heads.

BE CLEOPATRA FOR A DAY!

A great way to relax is to have a full ancient Egyptian make-over. Start your pampering with a bath. Servants will pour jugs of water or milk over your skin. Next you will be covered in perfumed oil – this helps to protect you from the sun. Then you can have your head shaved. The ancient Egyptians have excellent bronze razors. A special treatment for balding men is a scalp rub with snake or crocodile fat. Afterwards your eyes will be made up with kohl and eye shadow and your lips and nails will be dyed with bright red henna (a dye from plant leaves). Finally, you'll be able to choose a wig from a selection made from human hair or plant fibres.

WHAT TO EAT

Ancient Egyptian food is very healthy. You'll find plenty of fresh fruit, onions, green vegetables, fish, and lentils on the menu, and not much fat or sugar.

The basis of all meals is bread – the ancient Egyptians were the first civilization to use yeast to make their bread rise. Most people eat a kind of bread made without yeast called unleavened bread. It is similar to pitta bread. There are also delicious sweet breads which taste more like cake, such as bread sweetened with dates.

The ancient Egyptians use a selection of herbs and spices in their cooking, including rosemary, cinnamon, dill, cumin, and coriander. If you have a sweet tooth then honey is used instead of sugar.

In this model, bakers are hard at work kneading dough to make bread.

ROAST PELICAN AND PIGEON

Meat is a delicacy and expensive. The national dish is goose roasted over hot embers. It is usually eaten on special occasions, and then only by the rich or **elite**. Roast duck, beef, pigeon, and pelican are also popular. Pork is not a popular dish because some ancient Egyptians believe that pig meat carries **leprosy**. Meat and fish are often smoked or salted to preserve them.

WHAT TO DRINK

The water from the Nile can be brown and dirty, and is probably full of germs. But most local people drink it and survive to tell the tale. Beer is very popular and people often brew it at home, using barley or wheat. Ancient Egyptian beer is very different to the beer people drink today. It is thick, like a milkshake, and is supposed to be really good for you.

The ancient Egyptians make their own wine but there is also fine **imported** wine. Look for labels telling you about the wine – they tend to have no nonsense descriptions such as "good wine", "very very good wine" and "sweet wine" written on them. Also, try the selection of freshly squeezed fruit juices.

The Nile Valley is perfect for growing grapes. These are often used to make delicious local wine.

TABLE MANNERS

Most ancient Egyptians eat squatting on the ground or on mats. Don't worry about using cutlery though. They use their fingers to eat and water is poured over their hands after each course of the meal. Wealthy Egyptians often sit on low chairs or cushions next to small tables.

MONEY

If you visit during the New Kingdom, you will find that the ancient Egyptians do not use money. (Money is introduced by the Greeks during the Ptolemaic period: 332–330 BC.)

Usually, a person's wealth is measured by the number of cattle they own. Don't panic though – you won't need to take cattle with you all the way to ancient Egypt! Ancient Egyptians happily accept gold, other precious metals, grain, and oil in exchange for goods and services. Some people will also take cloth, jewellery, or everyday objects. Remember to pack some things from home that are not available in ancient Egypt, as these will be excellent for **bartering**.

PRICES

As there is no money it is difficult to give things a price. The ancient Egyptians price things by using copper weights or rings, called *debens* and *seniu*. If you're travelling during the New Kingdom you will also find gold, silver, and copper weights, called *kits*. Obviously, prices will vary depending on the period that you visit. During the New Kingdom, a sack of wheat weighing about 58 kg (128 lbs) is about two *deben* of copper. By the end of the period, during the reign of Ramesses XI, the value of an ox is about 5 kit of silver (or 60 *deben* of copper).

THE POSTAL SERVICE

Ancient Egyptians use symbols called **hieroglyphs** for writing. Scribes will take down your message on papyrus. The ancient Egyptians use messengers and soldiers to carry messages. They have also started a carrier pigeon service, where messages are flown by specially trained pigeons. Whatever method you choose, don't expect the service to be quick! The best way of sending a message in ancient Egypt is via the Nile and then by horseback.

> ↖ The grain harvested by hard-working slaves could be exchanged for other goods.

PAPERWORK

The ancient Egyptians love their paperwork. Scribes scribble away all day on papyrus, clay tablets, or on wall paintings. They enjoy taking memos, writing letters, journals, wills, lists of rules and regulations, journals, transcripts of meetings, and trials from the law courts. The ancient Egyptians are very organized. If you travel in the New Kingdom, expect to be delayed on your journey by filling in loads of forms.

PAPYRUS FOR PAPER

Papyrus is a tough, tall river reed that you will see growing along the banks of the Nile. The ancient Egyptians have found a way of crushing the stems to make a kind of paper, called papyrus. It is light and easier to transport than blocks of stone or clay. Papyrus reeds are also used to make sandals, boats, and rope.

A sailing boat is the best way to travel in ancient Egypt.

CHAPTER 3

TRAVEL, FOOD, AND SHELTER

Most ancient Egyptians live near the Nile and they get about on boats. You can expect to do very much the same on your visit, although horses are available if you can afford it. When it comes to accommodation in ancient Egypt, you will be relying upon the hospitality of the locals.

If you're lucky you might get a room for the night. Otherwise, you may get a blanket and a place to sleep on the roof under the stars.

TRAVELLING BY BOAT

The best way to travel between the major settlements along the Nile is, of course, by boat. And it is a wonderful experience! Boats travelling southwards use sails. The power of the north wind blows the sails and powers the boats upriver, against the current. Boats going north let the river do the work, though usually oars are needed to steer them.

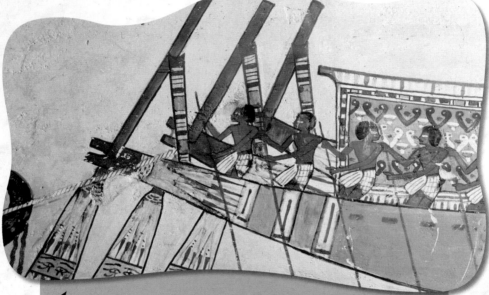

This barge is carrying a brightly painted shrine as part of a funeral ceremony.

Pharaohs and members of the royal family travel in magnificent barges. These have curved hulls and great, billowing rectangular sails. There are benches for the teams of oarsmen. These barges look majestic as they cut through the muddy waters of the Nile. If you plan to travel in style then this is the way to go.

HIEROGLYPHS TO REMEMBER

The picture of a ship with its sails billowing means "travelling south". The picture of a ship without a sail or mast means "travelling north".

RUSH HOUR ON THE NILE

If you are on a budget then the ancient Egyptians have excellent riverboats. These are mostly made from papyrus so they are light and glide through the water quickly. The river can get fairly busy carrying people and cargo. On your journeys you'll probably see plenty of big wooden barges carrying sculptures or great blocks of granite.

TRAVELLER'S TIPS

A good tip is to find a boat with a canopy to protect you from the fierce sunshine. But be warned! It can get very cold at night, so take a warm cloak. Also, prepare yourself for a long journey. A trip from the Nile Delta to Thebes can take eight or nine days. Because the Nile flows south to north, trips downriver (from south to north) are faster.

TRAVELLING BY LAND

With the world's longest river flowing the length of the country, there hasn't been a great rush to build a network of roads in ancient Egypt. For trips overland farmers and peasants tend to use donkeys and **mules**, while horses are ridden by the aristocracy. Don't expect to see any camels until about 525 BC, when the Persians invade and introduce this trusty animal.

If you have a lot of luggage then try to visit after the Second Intermediate Period (after 1550 BC), by which time the wheeled **chariot** has been invented. Then at least you will be able to hire a cart.

A pharaoh and groom sit on a chariot pulled by a pony.

WHERE TO STAY

In ancient Egypt many people have an open door policy, which means they will invite you to stay in their home. Of course, there is a big difference between a peasant's humble home and an aristocrat's luxury residence.

BUDGET BED AND BREAKFAST

Houses for workers and farmers are usually built of mud-brick. They are built close together, sometimes in terraces. You may be invited to sleep in a small room or even one of the store rooms. You'll probably have nothing more than a mat to sleep on.

Cooking takes place on the roof or in an unroofed room. If you are lucky there may be a toilet – a hole in the floor. The contents might be buried in a cesspit, otherwise they are dumped in the Nile. If there are no toilets then there may be a pot, or you'll need to find a hidden spot outside!

This model of an ordinary ancient Egyptian house is called a "soul house". It is home for a spirit in the Afterlife.

FIVE STAR ACCOMMODATION

If this sounds a bit rough then try to get an invitation to a bigger house. These are often painted white to deflect the heat. They usually have walled gardens, with trees and a pond. Inside, there are rooms for entertaining, cooking, and sleeping, as well as the servant's quarters and women's quarters.

Guests mostly stay on the first floor, while the owners stay on the floor above. The beds are made from wood and reeds, and are raised from the ground (away from creepy crawlies!). Strange wooden headrests are provided rather than pillows.

At the best homes there are en-suite bathrooms, and servants give showers by pouring jugfuls of water over you. The toilets are not too bad – a wooden or stone seat on a small platform above a pot. Windows and roof vents are positioned to take full advantage of the cooling north winds.

BOOK A TRIP TO AN OASIS

For the more adventurous there are **caravan** routes through the desert to the major **oases**. It takes weeks to reach one of these lush outposts. On the way you'll be camping out under the stars or in simple tents made from reeds and rough linen. Once you arrive you will be rewarded with excellent boating, swimming, fishing, and hunting. But watch out for hungry crocodiles and angry hippos!

The mysterious Sphinx watches over the great pyramids at Giza. It has a human head and a lion's body.

CHAPTER 4

PLACES TO VISIT

There are many wonderful places to visit in ancient Egypt. Most people who visit ancient Egypt think about the pyramids first, so a trip to Giza is a must for everyone. Some people can't wait to see the magnificent temples at Karnak, near Thebes. Don't let the fact that Giza and Thebes are hundreds of kilometres apart put you off visiting them both. Actually, it's quite easy to plan a trip that takes in most of the major tourist sites in ancient Egypt. Nearly all of them are beside the Nile, so it's possible to sail upriver (or paddle downriver!). You can stop off along the way and encounter all the treasures that ancient Egypt has to offer. Remember, you will have to barter with local boatmen, so take plenty of useful goods like fine cloth, jewels, and precious metal!

THE ROYAL CITY OF MEMPHIS

Memphis is a fashionable and exciting capital city located on the west bank of the Nile. It is a sprawling city that measures 30 kilometres (18.6 miles) from north to south. It is also a wonder of early engineering. The city is built on land that used to be flooded by the Nile. Now man-made **dykes** protect it from rising waters.

For an unusual day out you could visit the bird breeding grounds on the Memphis lakes. You'll see birds such as the ibis and falcon. When they are fully grown these birds will be mummified. The ancient Egyptians place mummified birds and animals in their tombs to keep them company in the Afterlife.

This fabulously decorated tomb of a vizier named Mereruka can be found in Saqqara.

TOP ATTRACTIONS IN MEMPHIS

- The Palace of Apries: impressive courtyard; throne room with beautiful limestone columns.
- The Temple of Ptah: you won't be able to see inside but it has a splendid **hypostyle** hall with rows of stone columns.
- Fine parks, gardens, and lakes found around the city.

CITY OF THE DEAD

A trip to Saqqara and Giza is the highlight of a visit to ancient Egypt. Saqqara and Giza are known as "the city of the dead", or **necropolis**. There are cemeteries, tombs, temples, and – of course – the pyramids, where the bodies of the dead pharaohs are laid to rest. The huge sloping sides of the pyramids are built as stairways to the sun for the pharaohs. The structures are solid except for a few chambers (rooms) where the body of the pharaoh and his belongings rest.

THE GREAT PYRAMID

A good time to visit is during the reign of Khufu of the Old Kingdom (2589–2566 BC). He is building the Great Pyramid at Giza as a stronghold for his body and a monument of his reign. His own mother's grave has been robbed, so he plans to make his Great Pyramid impossible to raid.

THE FIRST PYRAMID

Between the third and twelfth dynasties (2686–1795 BC) about 80 pyramids were built. The first pyramid to be built was "the step pyramid" at Saqqara. It gets its name because its sides are made of six giant steps. It was built for Pharaoh Djoser by his **architect** and vizier, Imhotep (see also page 56), around 2660 BC.

You will be able to see how the workers haul great chunks of stone across the desert using wooden rollers. When the Great Pyramid is finished it is called one of the seven wonders of the ancient world, so seeing how it is built is an opportunity not to be missed!

A TRIP DOWN THE NILE VALLEY

BENI HASAN

It is best to visit the necropolis Beni Hasan during the Middle Kingdom (2055–1650 BC) when the local rulers are building some exceptionally beautiful tombs. The tomb of Khnumhotep II, a local governor, has some of the most famous art in ancient Egypt, with many beautiful paintings of daily life. Meanwhile, at the tomb of Kheti you will see paintings of farming and wine-making.

THE ART OF THE WALL-PAINTER

This wall painting from the tomb of Khnumhotep II shows a slave harvesting figs. Ancient Egyptians have wall painting down to a fine art. First of all, stonemasons smooth the walls and apply a layer of plaster. Next the wall is divided into a grid using red paint. Then the scribes copy their sketched designs onto the walls using black paint. Next, the stonemasons chip out the important images, so they stand out from the background. Last of all the painters fill in the colours. The bright greens are made from powdered malachite. The deep red is made from iron oxide mixed with egg white and gum.

AKHETATEN

The city of Akhetaten was created for the New Kingdom ruler Amenhotep IV (1352–1336 BC), who started a new religion based on worshipping the god of the sun disc, Aten. As part of the new religion, Amenhotep changed his name to Akhenaten and built a city dedicated to Aten. However, this caused religious upheaval because most ancient Egyptians believe in many gods.

Akhetaten is only the capital city during the reign of King Akhenaten, so you have just fourteen years to visit! The city has many attractions. Unlike most other temples, the Great Temple of Aten has no roof so that sunlight floods into the temple.

Other attractions include the king's beautiful wife, Nefertiti. Rumour has it she is one of the most beautiful women in ancient Egypt. She is certainly one of the most powerful women, and you would be lucky to get a glimpse of her.

A famous face: Queen Nefertiti and her daughter worshipping the Sun god Aten.

ABYDOS

Abydos is a holy place in ancient Egypt and the centre of worship to the god of the dead, Osiris. You will see many people making a pilgrimage to the Temple of Osiris. Ancient Egyptians try to visit Abydos once in their lifetime. A good time to visit is during the Abydos Festival, which is held once a year. You will see plays of the story of Isis and Osiris, and pageants and processions. The town fizzes with celebration and excitement.

THEBES

Thebes is the capital city of the New Kingdom. It's like two towns in one city. On the east bank of the Nile is the thriving commercial city and the stunning temples of Karnak and Luxor. The west bank of the Nile is very different – it's a barren place with dry limestone hills. These dusty hilltops are the burial ground for the New Kingdom pharaohs. It is called the Valley of the Kings.

A magical view across the Sacred Lake of Amun, Karnak.

THE MAGIC OF KARNAK

You will need a few days to take in all the wonderful sites on the east bank of Thebes and the temples at Karnak. Together they form the largest temple complex in ancient Egypt. The three temple complexes include the temple to the god Amun, king of the gods, and two smaller temples dedicated to the gods Mut and Khonsu.

The Temple of Amun is approached from the Nile by an impressive avenue of **sphinxes** with rams' heads. The temple walls are decorated with painted scenes of everyday and religious life. Inside the temple, look out for the impressive **colossus** of Ramesses II. This giant granite statue stands at the entrance to the Great Hypostyle Hall. It was built by Sety I and finished by Ramesses II, so it might be best to plan your trip once Ramesses has completed it.

LUXOR

Luxor Temple is just 2 kilometres (1.2 miles) from Karnak. You can reach it by river or you might walk along the elegant avenue of sphinxes, which connect Karnak and Luxor. Luxor is also dedicated to the gods Amun, Mut, and Khonsu. It is much smaller than Karnak but has some equally grand attractions. At the entrance of the temple are two statues of Ramesses II. There is also a striking pair of pink granite obelisks. These reach 25 metres (82 feet) into the air and point towards the sun god, Re.

THE FESTIVAL OF OPET

If you want to see the ancient Egyptians letting their hair down, then head for Karnak during the Festival of Opet. The festival celebrates the king's rebirth as the son of Amun and takes place each year during the floods. Crowds of people line the banks of the Nile to watch the sacred statue of Amun being taken upriver by boat from Karnak to the temple at Luxor. Later, the pharaoh takes part in a special ceremony and everyone celebrates his god-like status.

The Sphinxes at Luxor. The human head represents intelligence and the lion's body symbolizes strength.

INTO THE VALLEY OF THE KINGS

Plan your day out at the Valley of Kings well. Go during the early morning or late afternoon, when the temperature is cooler. Take plenty of water and pack a scarf to protect yourself from the Sun. The dry limestone hills in the Valley of the Kings aren't welcoming, but this is why the pharaohs chose this place to be buried. They wanted somewhere remote, far away from grave robbers and other people, where they could truly rest in peace.

The death mask of Tutankhamen, buried within the tomb in the Valley of the Kings.

The Valley of the Kings is supposed to be a secret place. If you want to catch a glimpse of the treasures being taken to the tombs then plan your trip during the New Kingdom (1550–1069 BC) when the tombs are being built. Highlights include the tomb of Ramesses VI. It has a large arched roof that is decorated with the goddess Nut swallowing the sun. The tomb of the boy-king Tutankhamen is also worth a visit. His mummy is covered with a beautiful golden mask and he is buried with mountains of gold and precious jewels, childhood toys, baskets of fruit, and jars of wine.

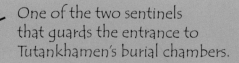

One of the two sentinels that guards the entrance to Tutankhamen's burial chambers.

At Deir-al-Bahn in Luxor stands the temple of Queen Hatshepsut, one of the few female Egyptian pharaohs. Much of the temple is destroyed by Ramesses II so plan a trip there before his reign.

TOP TOMBS

The Valley of the Kings has hundreds of tombs that have been cut into the cliffs. Some of these are very deep with stairs, hallways leading to burial chambers. A few tombs have false burial chambers to trick tomb robbers. Most of the tombs are decorated with wall-paintings that show the journey to the Afterlife. Nobles and other important people are also buried near the Valley of the Kings.

VALLEY OF THE QUEENS

Royal wives and children are laid to rest in the Valley of the Queens. It is rumoured that the most beautiful tomb in all ancient Egypt has been built here for Queen Nefertari, the favourite wife of Ramesses II. Wonderful wall-paintings show Nefertari on her journey to the Afterlife.

HOMES FOR THE WORKERS

A visit to Thebes would not be complete without a quick peek at Deir el-Medina. This new town has been built to house the builders and families of people working at the Valley of the Kings. It is cleverly designed with streets of terraced housing, shops, and businesses. There is also a fine temple dedicated to Hathor.

This colourful wall painting shows the nobleman Nebamun as he hunts for birds and fish on the Nile.

CHAPTER 5

THINGS TO DO

There's more to ancient Egypt than temples and tombs. Once you've done the sightseeing you might fancy some shopping. There are plenty of opportunities to snap up some bargains at the market place. The ancient Egyptians head for the Nile to swim, fish, and hunt. For your entertainment there are banquets with dancers, acrobats, and musicians. There are also plays at the temples and hockey matches in the towns. Highlights of the year are the festivals, such as the festival of Bastet, when all the locals parade in the street.

LET'S SHOP!

The market places of ancient Egypt are filled with fresh fish, fruit and vegetables, herbs and spices, and a delicious assortment of home-baked bread and home-brewed beer. If you're looking for local handicrafts then it may be better to visit local craftsmen. You should be able to find potters, carpenters, glassmakers, jewellers, weavers, and leatherworkers going about their business in most major towns.

BARTERING FOR BEGINNERS

If you're used to buying things with money then bartering for goods might feel a bit strange. It's good to have a rough idea of the value of the goods you wish to buy before you begin your shopping trip. Stallholders at the market usually weigh their produce using copper weights called *debens*. If you have a piece of linen worth 1 deben then it can be exchanged for goods worth 1 deben. With craftsmen it will be a matter of bargaining until you can agree upon an exchange you are both happy with.

The ancient Egyptians have a wide selection of interesting board games. Some are made in the shapes of animals, like this one.

WHAT TO BUY?

If you want a typically ancient Egyptian souvenir, then why not choose a board game like Senet (see box) or Hounds and Jackals? There are some lovely toys such as carved ivory animals, dolls, wooden animals (look out for crocodiles and leopards with mouths that snap shut), boats, and balls. You could also buy polished bronze or copper mirrors, fine linen, perfume oils, glassware, statuettes of gods and goddesses, and musical instruments.

BEAUTIFUL JEWELLERY

Ancient Egyptian jewellery is beautiful to look at and has hidden meaning too. People believe that certain precious jewels, gemstones, and metals can protect or bring good luck to the wearer. Lapis lazuli (a bright blue gemstone) and turquoise (a greenish-blue semi-precious stone) are thought to bring joy and delight. Gold is connected to the Sun, and copper is associated with the goddess Hathor. Note that silver is rarer than gold, so it is more expensive. Glass beads are also very popular.

THE MAGICAL GAME

The rules of the game of Senet are complicated. The board has 30 holes, 3 rows, and 10 columns. Each player has 5 or 7 pawns, sticks, or knucklebones. During the New Kingdom people believe a person's ability to play Senet symbolizes his or her passage to the Afterlife.

A LASTING MEMORY

Why not ask an artist to capture you or your family on papyrus? Ancient Egyptian artists have their own style. They paint eyes and shoulders as if they were seeing the person from the front and they paint the body side on, as in the picture on page 42.

TAKE ME TO THE RIVER

When it comes to having a good time, the Nile provides endless possibilities. There is excellent swimming and boating. Boat races and boat games are also popular. One game, in which two teams of men holding long poles attempt to push each other into the river, causes quite a splash! Fishing is common, as is hunting birds with throw-sticks (these are rather like extra large, lethal boomerangs), and crocodile and hippopotamus hunting can be arranged.

Slave girls entertain guests at a banquet with music and dancing.

There is hunting inland too. In the desert people trap animals such as hares, hyenas, gazelles, and foxes. If you travel to ancient Egypt from the time of the New Kingdom (1550–1069 BC), big-game hunting on chariots is also popular.

ENTERTAINMENT

Plays are sometimes performed at the temples. These "plays" are about religion and are nothing like the theatre you may be used to. People also enjoy watching a kind of ball game that is similar to hockey. Men use long palm tree branches for sticks and have a puck (hard disc) made from leather stuffed with papyrus.

LAVISH BANQUETS

Ancient Egyptian banquets are a must for any traveller. Most banquets are private parties hosted by the middle and upper classes. There is plenty of entertainment, with music, singing, dancing, jugglers, and acrobats. Servants will bring you the finest selection of food, and your cup will be regularly topped up with wine or beer. The ancient Egyptians like to get drunk and are regularly sick from too much alcohol.

FESTIVALS

The ancient Egyptian word for a party or holy day (holiday) is *heru-nefer*, which translates as "a good day". Festivals and holidays are an excuse for rich and poor to eat and drink too much, and enjoy music and dancing. The festivals to the lesser gods tend to be less serious and more fun. On the holy day of the cat goddess Bastet, no work is done and people parade in the streets wearing masks. The Beautiful Feast of the Valley is celebrated each year in Thebes. The highlight of the day is visiting the tombs of loved ones and eating a meal at the graveside.

HOW PECULIAR!
At some parties, servants put cones of perfumed grease on the heads of the guests. As the grease melts it runs down on to the guest's hair and face. This is supposed to cool the person down!

A nobleman, dressed in a panther skin, offers lotus and papyrus to the god Osiris.

HEALTH – WHAT TO EXPECT

Stomach upsets and diarrhoea are common in ancient Egypt. Most holidaymakers are poorly sometime during their visit. It's hardly surprising because people throw human waste outside their homes. Birds, animals, and insects feed on the rubbish and spread germs quickly. Eye infections and diseases are extremely common. Visitors can be badly affected by heat. Sunstroke and sunburn can ruin your holiday so take care in the Sun and stay in the shade if possible.

DEADLY DISEASES OF ANCIENT EGYPT

- **Cholera**: waterborne disease causing severe diarrhoea and vomiting.
- **Tuberculosis**: airborne disease which affects the lungs.
- **Smallpox**: highly contagious virus; causes spots on the skin which leave scars.
- **Bilharzia**: passed to humans by infected snails living in fresh water.
- **Malaria**: passed to humans by infected mosquitoes.

A VISIT TO THE DOCTOR

Ancient Egyptian doctors are possibly the best you will find in the ancient world. They know a lot about the human body and how it works. This knowledge probably comes from their experience of removing organs and embalming bodies for mummification. Ancient Egyptian surgeons have even attempted brain surgery.

However, the ancient Egyptians haven't quite mastered medicine. They think that the heart is used for thinking and don't know what the brain is used for. But don't let this worry you, as most doctors use their common sense. They only turn to magic and religion if they can't find a cure. Be prepared for a doctor to ask you some rather strange questions, though. Many doctors believe that dreams can hold the answer to the state of your health.

FIGHTING SICKNESS

Medicine and treatments can be anything from very good to downright peculiar. Eye infections are helped by applying a mixture of honey and ochre to the eyes using a vulture **quill** for a dropper. But it's probably best to avoid cures such as water from pigs' eyes or tortoise bile (digestive juices).

Honey is commonly used as an antiseptic to kill germs and bacteria, and does seem to help minor cuts and wounds to heal. Some doctors will apply raw meat to a bad wound, which they say helps to stop the bleeding. Broken bones are set using wooden splints or palm ribs.

A doctor attends to a patient with an eye problem.

COMMON ANCIENT EGYPTIAN CURES
- **To stop diarrhoea**: take one-eighth of a cup of figs and grapes, bread dough, corn, fresh earth, onion, and elderberry.
- **To cure indigestion**: crush a hog's tooth and put inside four sugar cakes. Eat one cake a day for four days.
- **To ease pain**: anoint the body (cover in oil) and expose to the Sun.

SECURITY

Ancient Egypt is one of the safest places in the ancient world for travellers. People don't use money or carry wallets and purses, so there is little threat from pickpockets. As most of your travel is by boat on the Nile you won't need to keep a look out for bandits hiding in the hills. Ancient Egypt is also safe because people have strong religious beliefs (see pages 14–15). Most people try to be honest because that is the best way of pleasing the goddess Ma'at.

BEWARE OF THIEVES!

Even though you are quite safe in ancient Egypt, it is best to be on your guard. Thieves may try to steal your luggage, and there will always be people who try to take advantage of you.

One of the biggest crimes in ancient Egypt is tomb robbery. This is so common that it is regarded as a "profession". Tomb robbers usually work in teams and steal from royal tombs. They can take everything from the fine jewellery and precious items buried with the mummy, to the gold fittings on the sarcophagus.

A TIME TO AVOID!

Don't travel to ancient Egypt during the first Intermediate Period [2181–2055 BC]. Here is a news report from the day: "Behold, the land is full of gangs and the farmer goes to plough with his shield... crime is everywhere... wearers of fine linen are beaten with sticks... Behold, things are done that were never done before and the king has been robbed by beggars." (From *The Admonitions of Ipuwer/ Judgement of the Pharaoh* by Joyce Tyldesley.)

↑ These men are being led off to be punished for not working hard enough!

PUNISHMENT

It takes a brave person to rob a royal tomb. He is disobeying the pharaoh and displeasing the gods. The penalty for this is high. The sentence for tomb robbery is death by impalement. This means that the guilty person is lowered on to a sharp stake and left to die very slowly. The robber is also so badly beaten that his body is no use to him in the Afterlife (a terrible fate for any ancient Egyptian).

For petty crimes people are beaten, whipped, branded, or have their ears and nose cut off. The police and tax collectors regularly use leather batons and sticks too. There are prisons, but ancient Egyptians prefer their punishments to be painful and quick.

Hieroglyphs are believed to be the first writing system in the world.

CHAPTER 7

ANCIENT EGYPT FACTS AND FIGURES

This final section is an easy reference guide for the time traveller. Check out "Ancient Egypt at a glance" to find out the major periods and royal dynasties of ancient Egypt. This chapter gives you a quick list of some of the great people and celebrities – royal and otherwise – to look out for. No trip to a foreign land is complete without a phrase book. In ancient Egypt people use "picture words" called hieroglyphs. They are often beautiful to look at but can be very difficult to understand, so a selection of common words and their meanings is given in this section.

ANCIENT EGYPTIAN PHRASE BOOK

The ancient Egyptians use picture writing called hieroglyphs for tomb wall paintings and temples. There are several thousand hieroglyphs so it is a difficult language to master. However, hieroglyphs are extremely beautiful, almost like works of art. The hieroglyphs can be read vertically and horizontally. Scribes also use a kind of shorthand of hieroglyphs called hieratic writing.

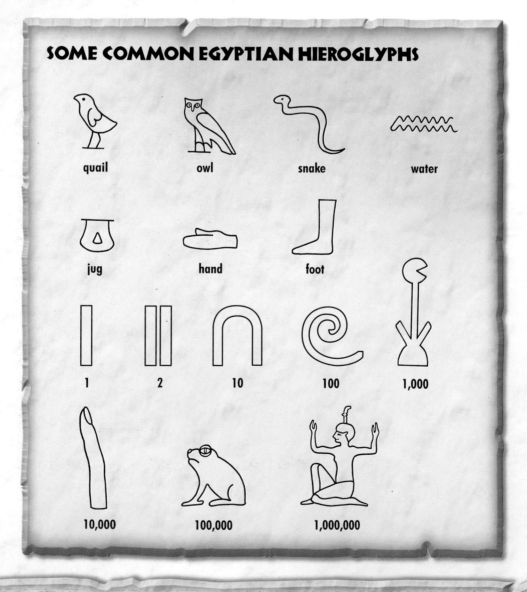

SOME COMMON EGYPTIAN HIEROGLYPHS

quail

owl

snake

water

jug

hand

foot

1

2

10

100

1,000

10,000

100,000

1,000,000

USEFUL EGYPTIAN WORDS AND PHRASES

(Pronunciation is in *italics*)

I = *inek*
my = say *ee* after the word
My name is … = *ren-ee* …

Hello = *hee*
Good morning = *sebat neferet*
Good evening = *masheru nefer*

Where (is…)? = *chen…?*
How much (is…)? = *wer…?*
I want, I would like = *mer-ee*

this = *pen*
that = *pef*
there = *im*

water = *mu*
bread = *ta*
figs = *daby*
fish = *rem*
meat = *iwef*
food = *wenemet*
eat = *wenem*
drink = *sewary*

I am/we are hungry = *inek/inu heker*
I am/we are thirsty = *inek/inu ibu*
chariot = *wereret*
to sail south = *henet*
to sail north = *hed*
to sail across = *wedja*
to go = *shem*
Do you go to… = *shem-tenu en…*

bad = *bin*
good = *nefer*
a little (of) = *nehy (en)*

one = *wat*
two = *senu*
ten = *medju*
many = *asha*

today = *hen*
tomorrow = *miseba*
yes = *chew*
no = *nen*

ANCIENT EGYPT AT A GLANCE

TIMELINE

(Please note that dates are approximate.)

5500–3000 BC   **PRE-DYNASTIC PERIOD**
The beginning of hieroglyphic writing

3100–2686 BC   **EARLY DYNASTIC PERIOD**
The creation of the Egyptian state in about 3250 BC.

3100–2890	1st Dynasty
3100	Narmer (Menes)
2890–2686	2nd Dynasty

2686–2181 BC   **OLD KINGDOM**
The Great Pyramids at Giza are built.

2686–2613	3rd Dynasty
2686–2667	Sanakht
2667–2648	Djoser
2613–2498	4th Dynasty
2613–2589	Sneferu
2589–2566	Khufu
2558–2532	Khafra
2494–2345	5th Dynasty
2345–2181	6th Dynasty

2181–2055 BC   **FIRST INTERMEDIATE PERIOD**
Egypt is divided into two states, with a northern capital at Memphis and a southern capital at Thebes. (Thebes was the only capital during the 11th Dynasty.)

2181–2125	7th and 8th Dynasties
2160–2025	9th and 10th Dynasties
2125–2055	11th Dynasty

2055–1650 BC   **MIDDLE KINGDOM**
The country is reunited by the pharaoh Mentuhotep II; the Classical period of art and literature.

2055–1985	11th Dynasty
2055–2004	Mentuhotep II
1985–1795	12th Dynasty
1985–1955	Amenemhat I
1795–1650	13th and 14th Dynasties

1650–1550 BC   SECOND INTERMEDIATE PERIOD
15th, 16th and 17th Dynasties. Dates from this period are uncertain. Ancient Egypt is ruled by the Hykos until Egyptian rulers drive them out and begin the 17th Dynasty.

1550–1069 BC   NEW KINGDOM
Often described as the golden age of ancient Egypt. The second half of the 18th Dynasty and beginning of the 19th Dynasty are a good time to visit ancient Egypt. Building work starts at the Valley of the Kings.

1550–1295	18th Dynasty
	Ahmose
1525–1504	Amenhotep I
1473–1458	Queen Hatshepsut
1427–1400	Amenhotep II
1352–1336	Amenhotep IV (Akhenaten)
1336–1327	Tutankhamen
1323–1295	Horemheb
1295–1186	19th Dynasty
1295–1294	Ramesses I
1294–1279	Sety I
1279–1213	Ramesses II
1186–1069	20th Dynasty

1069–747 BC   THIRD INTERMEDIATE PERIOD
Ancient Egypt loses power and is taken over by Nubian rulers. 21st, 22nd, 23rd, 24th Dynasties rule the country.

747–332 BC   LATE PERIOD
The Assyrians and Persians rule over ancient Egypt. 25th, 26th, 27th, 28th, 29th and 30th Dynasties rule the country.

332–305 BC   THE MACEDONIANS
Alexander the Greek conquers ancient Egypt in 332.

305–30 BC   THE PTOLEMAIC DYNASTY
A troubled time which begins with the rule of Ptolemy I, a general of Alexander the Great.

51–30	Queen Cleopatra.
30	Egypt becomes part of the Roman Empire.

GREAT ANCIENT EGYPTIANS

- **Imhotep** (around 2675 BC) – designed what was probably the first pyramid – the Step Pyramid at Saqqara (see page 35).
- **Khufu** (around 2589–2566 BC) – a strong and possibly cruel leader, Khufu's kingdom was so strong that his country was never attacked from outside. Khufu is famous for building the Great Pyramid at Giza.
- **Tutankhamen** (died circa 1325 BC) – became pharaoh when he was just 9 years old. He died aged about 18. Some people believe that he was murdered but there is no proof.
- **Ramesses II** (circa 1279–1213 BC) – also known as Ramesses the Great, this mighty pharaoh ruled ancient Egypt for 66 years. He was a military man who defeated the Hittites at the Battle of Qadesh in about 1274 BC. His interest in building was well known. Amongst his finest buildings are the Great Temple at Abu Simbel, the colonnaded hall at the Karnak Temple, and the **mortuary** temple of his father Sety I at Thebes.

CLEOPATRA: THE LAST RULER OF ANCIENT EGYPT

Cleopatra VII (circa 51–30 BC) took the throne aged 19, sharing it with her younger brother, Ptolemy XIII. However, Ptolemy plotted to rule Egypt without her and Cleopatra was forced into exile. At the time, the Roman Empire was more powerful than Egypt, so Cleopatra made an alliance with a Roman general called Julius Caesar. Caesar drove Ptolemy out and Cleopatra regained her throne. Later, Cleopatra gave birth to Caesar's son, Caesarion, and visited him in Rome. Caesar was assassinated in 44 BC, and Cleopatra returned to Egypt, ruling with her son.

In 41 BC, Cleopatra formed a relationship with the Roman leader Mark Antony. Mark Antony was to marry Cleopatra and live in Egypt. This made him unpopular at home and in 32 BC, the Roman Empire declared war on Egypt. After losing a critical battle, Mark Antony committed suicide and Cleopatra was captured. She is said to have killed herself by getting an asp (a snake) to bite her. She was the last ruler of ancient Egypt before it became part of the mighty Roman Empire.

FURTHER READING

BOOKS

Amazing Facts about Ancient Egypt, James Putnam and Jeremy Pemberton (Thames and Hudson, 1994)

Ancient Egypt: Eyewitness Guide, George Hart (Dorling Kindersley, 2002)

The Awesome Egyptians (Horrible History series), Terry Deary and Martin Brown (Scholastic, 1993)

Encyclopedia of Ancient Egypt (Usborne Publishing Ltd, 2004)

Hieroglyph Handbook: Teach Yourself Ancient Egyptian, Philip Ardagh (Faber and Faber, 1999)

WEBSITES

- http://www.guardians.net/egypt/kids/ – An excellent list of links to children-friendly sites.
- http://www.ancientegypt.co.uk/menu.html – The website for the British Museum.
- http://www.nationalgeographic.com/media/tv/mumquiz/ mummyquiz1.html – A quick quiz to find out just how much you know about how to make a mummy.

GLOSSARY

Afterlife place where ancient Egyptians believed the dead went

amulets good luck charms, often worn as jewellery

architect person who designs buildings

aristocracy highest social rank in society, the nobility

barter to trade by exchanging food or other goods rather than using money

capital most important city in a country. It is usually the centre of government.

caravan number of travellers and camels crossing a desert together

chariot small, two-wheeled cart that is pulled by a horse or mule

chief justice the leading judge in a court of law

colossus statue which is much bigger than life size

delta area where a river begins to spread out into several channels before it reaches the sea

dyke long wall or embankment which is built to stop flooding, especially from rivers or the sea

elite top rank of society

embalm to treat a dead body with spices and oils to stop it from decaying

empire group of countries or lands that are controlled by one ruler

faith healing way of healing a person using faith and trust, often in religion, rather than medicine

fertile something that is rich and full of goodness. Fertile land is good for growing plants and crops

hieroglyphs symbols and pictures that are used in ancient Egyptian writing

high priest chief priest who worked in a temple serving the gods and goddesses

Hyksos group of foreign people, probably from Palestine or Syria

hypostyle great hall with a roof that is supported by rows of stone columns

import to bring foreign goods into another country

leprosy skin disease which can cause parts of skin and limbs to rot away

mortuary room or building where dead bodies are kept until they are buried

mule offspring of a female horse and a male donkey

mummification the process of preserving a dead body by embalming and wrapping it in bandages

necropolis ancient cemetery or burial place

oasis fertile area in the desert with its own natural source of water

papyrus reed that the ancient Egyptians made into paper

plague deadly disease which spreads quickly over a wide area

quill hollow stem of a bird's feather, used as a pen

sarcophagus stone coffin which is often decorated with sculptures or carved inscriptions

scribe person whose job it is to copy books or documents by hand

shrine place that is sacred to a god or holy person

silt fertile mud washed up from the riverbed during floods

sphinx stone sculpture with a lion's body and a human head

vizier chief advisor to the pharaoh

INDEX